I0415250

Quote It On

By Nataliia S. Ribeiro

Disclaimer: While all attempts have been made to verify the information provided in this publication author assumes any responsibility for errors, omissions, or contrary interpretations of the subject matter herein. This book is for entertainment purpose only and should not be taken as expert instruction or commands. The Reader is responsible for his or her own actions.

Adherence to all applicable laws and regulations, including international, federal, state, and local governing professional licensing, business practices, advertising and all other aspects of doing business in the UK, USA or any other jurisdiction is the sole responsibility of the purchaser or reader. The author assumes no responsibilities or liability whatsoever on the behalf of the purchaser or reader of this materials

Quote It On, London 2018.

Introduction

"One must be careful of books, and what is inside them, for words have the power to change us." – Cassandra Clare.

It is so true that words have the power to change us, they can inspire and motivate us, they can help us to change our lives for the better.

How often do you need some inspiration and motivation in your life? This collection of inspirational and motivational quotes will give you some inspiration and motivation as often as you read it.

This quotations book with the best selection of quotes ranging from Socrates to Captain Jack Sparrow was designed to make the readers stay positive 365+1 days or even more.

Be positive and Quote It On!

Quote it on

The secret of success is consistency of purpose.
— Benjamin Disraeli

The future belongs to those who believe in the beauty of their dreams.
— Franklin D. Roosevelt

We become what we think about most of the time, and that's the strangest secret.
— Earl Nightingale

If you don't design your own life plan, chances are you'll fall into someone else's plan. And guess what they have planned for you? Not much.
— Jim Rohn

Start by doing what's necessary; then do what's possible; and suddenly you are doing the impossible.
— Francis of Assisi

Karma has no menu, you get served what you
deserve.
— Bill Murray

It's not what you look at that matters, it's what
you see.
— Unknown

Make the most of the best and the least of the
worst.
— Robert Louis Stevenson

Never apologize to others for their
misunderstanding of who you are.
— Unknown

Other people's opinion of you does not have to
become your reality.
— Les Brown

One of the best ways to influence people is to
make them feel important.
— Roy T. Bennett

Someone has to write all those stories: why not
me?
— Elizabeth Gilbert

Talk low, talk slow, and don't say too much.
— John Wayne

Never cut what you can untie.
— Joseph Joubert

Only put off until tomorrow what you are willing
to die having left undone.
— Pablo Picasso

Hardships often prepare ordinary people for an
extraordinary destiny.
— C.S. Lewis

If you can dream it, you can do it.
— Walt Disney

To reach a great height a person needs to have
great depth.
— Unknown

We are what we repeatedly do. Excellence, then, is not an act, but a habit.
— Aristotle

Don't let the fear of losing be greater than the excitement of winning.
— Robert Kiyosaki

Success doesn't come to you, but you go to it.
— Marva Collins

Always be kinder than you feel.
— Unknown

Build your own dreams, or someone else will hire you to build theirs.
— Farrah Gray

Love is not only something you feel, it is something you do.
— David Wilkerson

Don't let someone dim your light simply because it's shining in their eyes.
— Jessica Ainscough

A pessimist sees the difficulty in every opportunity; an optimist sees the opportunity in every difficulty.
— Winston Churchill

Patience is bitter, but its fruit is sweet.
— Jean-Jacques Rousseau

To accomplish great things, we must not only act, but also dream, not only plan, but also believe.
— Anatole France

There are those who make things happen. There are those who watch things happen, and there are those who wonder what happened.
— Jim Lovell

Don't wish for it, work for it.
— Unknown

Do not be afraid of that which should be afraid of you.
— Constance Friday

Don't stop until you are proud.
— Unknown

The measure of who we are is what we do with
what we have.
— Vince Lombardi

Don't ever let anyone steal your dream. It's your
dream, not theirs.
— Dan Zadra

Forever is composed of nows.
— Emily Dickinson

A clever person solves a problem. A wise person
avoids it.
— Albert Einstein

Either you run the day, or the day runs you.
— Jim Rohn

Motivation is what gets you started. Habit is
what keeps you going.
— Jim Ryun

Most of the shadows of this life are caused by
our standing in our own sunshine.
— Ralph Waldo Emerson

Cancel your subscription if you are done with
someone's issues.
— Unknown

Rule your mind or it will rule you.
— Horace

Great people do things before they are ready.
— Amy Poehler

Don't be afraid to give up the good to go for the
great.
— John D. Rockefeller

Attract them by the way you live.
— Saint Augustine

Sometimes things become possible if we want
them bad enough.
— T.S. Eliot

Happiness is having a scratch for every itch.
— Ogden Nash

Somewhere, something incredible is waiting to
be known.
— Carl Sagan

Travel is the only thing you buy makes you
richer.
— Unknown

Success is walking from failure to failure with no
loss of enthusiasm.
— Winston Churchill

We are what we believe we are.
— C. S. Lewis

Difficult roads always lead to the beautiful
destination.
— Zig Ziglar

You have to risk going too far to discover just
how far you can really go.
— Jim Rohn

If you want to be seen, stand up. If you want to be heard, speak up. If you want to be appreciated, shut up.
— Bill Cosby

Inside of every problem lies an opportunity.
— Robert Kiyosaki

My silence could mean you are not worth the argument.
— Unknown

Let the beauty of what you love be what you do.
— Rumi

If you focus on results, you'll never change. If you focus on change, you'll get results.
— Jack Dixon

You must expect great things of yourself before you can do them.
— Michael Jordan

Silence is one of the great arts of conversation.
— Marcus Tullius Cicero

Don't let your loyalty become slavery.
— Karen Salmansohn

Do not dwell in the past, do not dream of the future, concentrate the mind on the present moment.
— Budha

Life is really simple, but we insist on making it complicated.
— Confucius

The time is always right to do what is right.
— Martin Luther King

People become successful the minute they decide to.
— Harvey Mackay

Live and learn.
— Unknown

He who hesitates is not only lost, but miles from the next exit.
— Ian Mcewan

If you want something you never had, you have to do something you've never done.
— Thomas Jefferson

Be fearless in the pursuit of what sets your soul on fire.
— Jennifer Lee

Grow wherever life puts you down.
— Ben Okri

A successful man is one who can lay a firm foundation with the bricks others have thrown at him.
— David Brinkley

Surround yourself with those who bring out the best in you, not the stress in you.
— Unknown

Believe in yourself. You are braver than you think, more talented than you know, and capable of more than you imagine.
— Roy T. Bennett

Live without pretending, Love without
depending, listen without defending, Speak
without offending.
— Drake

Good things happen in your life when you
surround yourself with positive people.
— Roy T. Bennett

It's often the last key on the ring that opens the
door.
— Paulo Coelho

Courage is what it takes to stand up and speak.
Courage is also what it takes to sit down and
listen.
— Winston Churchill

Accept no one's definition of your life; define
yourself.
— Harvey Fierstein

Build your own dreams, or someone else will
hire you to build theirs.
— Farrah Gray

Failure is the condiment that gives success its flavour.
— Truman Capote

If you can't excel with talent, triumph with effort.
— Stephen G. Weinbaum

More smiling, less worrying. More compassion, less judgment. More blessed, less stressed. More love, less hate.
— Roy T. Bennett

I can't change the direction of the wind, but I can adjust my sails to always reach my destination.
— Jimmy Dean

Think outside the box.
— Unknown

Make improvements, not excuses. Seek respect, not attention.
— Roy T. Bennett

Sometimes you have to walk away from what you want to find what you deserve.
— Belle Aurora

The day will happen whether or not you get up.
— John Ciardi

Be yourself, inspire the others.
— Oscar Wilde

Do not judge my story by the chapter you walked in on.
— Unknown

Do your best and forget the rest.
— Tony Horton

Everybody is a genius. But if you judge a fish by its ability to climb a tree, it will live its whole life believing that it is stupid.
— Albert Einstein

You don't have to be great to start, but you need to start to be great.
— Zig Ziglar

Make peace with your past so it doesn't spoil
your present.
— Denise Austin

The best way to get something done is to begin.
— Unknown

Be the part of the solution, not the problem.
— Stephen Covey

Keep putting out good; it will come back to you
tenfold in unexpected ways.
— Farrah Gray

No amount of regretting can change the past,
and no amount of worrying can change the
future.
— Roy T. Bennett

Don't compare your life with others, you have
no idea what their journey is all about.
— Regina Brett

Let your haters be your motivators.
— Nikki Carter

All men should strive to learn before they die,
what they are running from, and to, and why.
— James Thurber

You have to learn the rules of the game. And
then you have to play better than anyone else.
— Albert Einstein

Happiness is not something you postpone for
the future; it is something you design for the
present.
– Jim Rohn

What seems to us as bitter trials are often
blessings in disguise.
— Oscar Wilde

Always look for the fool in the deal. If you don't
find one, it's you.
— Mark Cuban

It is better to be a failure at something you love
than to be a success at something you hate.
— George Burns

Remember that not getting what you want is sometimes a wonderful stroke of luck.
— Dalai Lama

Don't ever take a fence down until you know why it was put up.
— Robert Frost

You are never too old to set another goal or to dream a new dream.
— C.S. Lewis

Fortune sides with him who dares.
— Virgil

Never complain and never explain.
— Benjamin Disraeli

Sometimes the place you are used to is not the place you belong.
— Queen of Katwe

It does not matter how slowly you go as long as you do not stop.
— Confucius

Grow through what you go through.
— Unknown

If you change nothing, nothing will change.
— Tony Robbins

The less you respond to negativity, the more
peaceful your life becomes.
— Unknown

Believe in yourself and you will be unstoppable.
— Emily Guay

Every story has three sides to it- yours, mine,
and the facts.
— Foster Meharry Russell

Start where you are. Use what you have. Do
what you can.
— Arthur Ashe

It's not the load that breaks you down, it's the
way you carry it.
— Lou Holtz

Trust yourself, then you will know how to live.
— Johann Wolfgang van Goethe

Don't try to be perfect. Just try to be better than you were yesterday.
– Unknown

Everything you can imagine is real.
— Pablo Picasso

Learn from the past, prepare for the future, and perform in the moment.
— Mike Van Hoozer

Always show the you in you, that makes you the you that you are.
— Sukh Sandu

One small crack does not mean that you are broken, it means that you were put to the test and you didn't fall apart.
— Linda Poindexter

Whatever you're thinking, think bigger.
— Tony Hsieh

He who dares, wins.
— Winston Churchill

Old ways will not open new doors.
— Unknown

Character consists of what you do on the third
and fourth tries.
— James A. Michener

Never let a problem to be solved become more
important than a person to be loved.
— Barbara Johnson

Arriving at one goal is the starting point to
another.
— John Dewey

Follow the dreams they know the way.
— Kobi Yamada

What lies behind you and what lies in front of
you, pales in comparison to what lies inside of
you.
— Ralph Waldo Emerson

Quiet people have the loudest minds.
— Stephen Hawking

Happiness is not by chance, but by choice.
— Jim Rohn

People only see what they prepared to see.
— Ralph Waldo Emerson

The meaning of life is to find your gift. The
purpose of life is to give it away.
— Unknown

Do not waste words on people who deserve
your silence.
— Mandy Hale

Do it now! Today will be yesterday tomorrow.
— Unknown

Most of the important things in the world have
been accomplished by people who have kept on
trying when there seemed to be no hope at all.
— Dale Carnegie

People are more what they hide than what they show.
— Pravinee Hurbungs

Try not to become just a man of success, but rather try to become a man of value.
— Albert Einstein

Be smart enough to hold on, be brave enough to let go.
— Unknown

Never let what you cannot do, stop you from doing what you can do.
— Ronald Reagan

Action expresses priorities.
— Mahatma Gandhi

Your ability will grow to match your dreams.
— Jim Rohn

Everything you've ever wanted is on the other side of fear.
— George Addair

If you can't explain it simply, you don't
understand it well enough.
— Albert Einstein

Normality is a paved road: it's comfortable to
walk, but no flowers grow.
— Vincent van Gogh

The distance between insanity and genius is
measured only by success.
— Bruce Feirstein

Make each day your masterpiece.
— John Wooden

Sometimes good things fall apart, so better
things can fall together.
— Marilyn Monroe

Inhale the future, exhale the past.
— Unknown

Do what you can with what you have, where
you are.
— Theodore Roosevelt

Always do right. This will gratify some people
and astonish the rest.
— Mark Twain

Go confidently in the direction of your dreams.
Live the life you have imagined.
— Henry David Thoreau

The quieter you become, the more you can
hear.
— Ram Dass

Let your speech be better than silence or be
silent.
— Dionysius I of Syracuse

If you can't make it good, at least make it look
good.
— Bill Gates

Failures are the stairs we climb to reach success.
— Roy T. Bennett

If you're going through hell, keep going.
— Winston Churchill

A goal is a dream with a deadline.
— Napoleon Hill

When it rains, look for rainbows. When it's dark,
look for stars.
— Oscar Wilde

If you don't fit in you are probably doing the
right thing.
— Unknown

Life is the art of drawing without an eraser.
— John W. Gardner

Nothing worth having comes easy.
— Theodore Roosevelt

Distance sometimes lets you know who's worth
keeping and who's worth letting go.
— Lana Del Rey

There are only two ways to live your life. One is
as though nothing is a miracle. The other is as
though everything is a miracle.
— Albert Einstein

Learn the rules like a pro, so you can break them
like an artist.
— Pablo Picasso

Never run back to whatever broke you.
— Unknown

Half of being smart is knowing what you are
dumb at.
— Solomon Short

Victory is always possible for the person who
refuses to stop fighting.
— Napoleon Hill

Stay away from negative people they have a
problem for every solution.
— Albert Einstein

Every exit is an entry to somewhere else.
— Tom Stoppard

The best way to gain self-confidence is to do
what you are afraid to do.
— Swati Sharma

Don't get burned twice by the same flame.
— Unknown

When writing the story of your life don't let
anyone else hold the pen.
— Harley Davidson

It's always too early to quit.
— Norman Vincent Peale

Everything starts as somebody's dream.
— Larry Niven

Tell me and I forget, teach me and I remember,
involve me and I learn.
—Benjamin Franklin

If you refuse to accept anything but the best,
you often get it.
— W. Somerset Mangham

Sometimes it takes sadness to know happiness,
noise to appreciate silence and absence to value
presence.
— Unknown

Life is not about getting and having it's about giving and being.
— Kevin Kruse

Don't think you are, know you are!
— Morpheus, in the film Matrix

Life can only be understood backwards, but it must be lived forwards.
—Soren Kierkegaard

By the time you know what it's all about, it's about all over.
— Unknown

Those who don't believe in magic will never find it.
— Roald Dahl

Time you enjoy wasting isn't wasted.
— John Lennon

If you are not willing to risk the usual you will have to settle for the ordinary.
— Jim Rohn

If you want to make a permanent change, stop focusing on the size of your problems and start focusing on the size of you!
—T. Harv Eker

Don't be afraid to fail be afraid not to try.
— Michael Jordan

Don't be pushed around by the fears in your mind. Be led by the dreams in your heart.
— Roy T. Bennett

Change your thoughts and you change your world.
— Norman Vincent Peale

If you can't do great things do small things in a great way.
— Napoleon Hill

There is a beauty in simplicity.
— Unknown

When nothing is sure, everything is possible.
— Margaret Drabble

Things work out best for those who make the
best of how things work out.
— John Wooden

Life isn't about finding yourself. Life is about
creating yourself.
— G.B. Shaw

Surround yourself with people who believe in
your dreams.
— Roy T. Bennett

Don't call it a dream call it a plan.
— Unknown

Change the way you look at things and the
things you look at change.
— Wayne Dyer

Don't be afraid to give up the good and go for
the great.
— John D. Rockefeller

Reading is a dreaming with open eyes.
— Yoyo

It is better to fail in originality than to succeed in imitation.
— Herman Melville

To have what you have never had, you have to do what you have never done.
— Thomas Jefferson

It is never too late to be what you might have been.
— George Eliot

Whatever you hold in your mind on a consistent basis is exactly what you will experience in your life.
— Tony Robbins

The best dreams happen when you are awake.
— Cherie Gilderbloom

It doesn't matter if it's a relationship a lifestyle or a job. If it doesn't make you happy let it go.
— Unknown

The most effective way to do it is to do it.
— Amelia Earhart

Treat everyone with politeness and kindness,
not because they are nice, but because you are.
— Roy T. Bennett

Our greatest glory is not in never falling, but in
rising every time we fall.
— Confucius

Don't stress. Do your best. Forget the rest.
— Unknown

Challenges are what make life interesting and
overcoming them is what makes life meaningful.
— Joshua Marine

Whatever the mind can conceive and believe, it
can achieve.
— Napoleon Hill

Success is liking yourself, liking what you do, and
liking how you do it.
— Maya Angelou

There is always a better way.
— Thomas Edison

Your mood should not dictate your manners.
— Unknown

Do not listen with the intent to reply, but with the intent to understand.
— Stephen R. Covey

Be happy in the moment, that's enough. Each moment is all we need, not more.
— Mother Teresa

Quality is not an act it is a habit.
— Aristotle

You can't make footprints in the sands of time if you're sitting on your butt. And who wants to make buttprints in the sands of time?
— Bob Moawad

Sometimes you have to lose the battle to win the war.
— Sun Tzu

Begin with the end in mind.
— Stephen Covey

Do not let the roles you play in life make you forget who you are.
— Roy T. Bennett

If you want to achieve greatness stop asking for permission.
— Unknown

Minds are like parachutes-they only function when open.
— Thomas Dewar

Dreams don't work unless you do.
— John C. Maxwell

Definiteness of purpose is the starting point of all achievement.
— W. Clement Stone

There is only one thing that makes a dream impossible to achieve: the fear of failure.
— Paulo Coelho

It's always seems impossible until it's done.
— Nelson Mandela

Do it with passion or not at all.
— Rosa Nochette Carey

Most of us are just about as happy as we make
up our minds to be.
— Abraham Lincoln

Don't raise your voice, improve your argument.
— Desmond Tutu

Let your dreams stay big and your worries stay
small.
— Unknown

The best way out is always through.
— Robert Frost

Don't be afraid of your fears. They're not there
to scare you. They're there to let you know that
something is worth it.
— C. JoyBell C.

At one point in your life you either have the
thing you want or the reasons why you don't.
— Andy Roddick

Never hope for it more than you work for it.
— Rita Mae Brown

Don't complain about the things you're not
willing to change.
— Andre Bramble

I am making changes in my life, so if you don't
hear from me, you are one of them.
— Unknown

Logic will get you from A to Z; imagination will
get you everywhere.
— Albert Einstein

Education breeds confidence.
— Confucius

The height of your accomplishments will equal
the depth of your convictions.
— William F. Scolavino

The price of greatness is responsibility.
— Winston Churchill

If you really want to do something, you will find a way. If you don't you'll find an excuse.
— Jim Rohn

To be old and wise, you must first have to be young and stupid.
— Unknown

Stop doing what is easy. Start doing what is right.
— Roy T. Bennett

Great minds discuss ideas; average minds discuss events; small minds discuss people.
— Eleanor Roosevelt

We do not see things as they are. We see things as we are.
— Rabbi Shemuel

Accept the past for what it was. Acknowledge the present for what it is. Anticipate the future for what it can become.
— Tracy L. McNair

All our dreams can come true if we have the courage to pursue them.
— Walt Disney

Do what you love, love what you do.
— Ray Bradbury

Good, better, best. Never let it rest. Till your good is better and your better is best.
— St. Jerome

The man who removes a mountain begins by carrying away small stones.
— William Faulkner

Ignore the noise and follow your choice.
— Unknown

The future belongs to those who see possibilities before they become obvious.
— John Scully

There are years that ask questions and years that answer.
— Zora Neale Hurston

Do not go where the path may lead, go instead
where there is no path and leave a trail.
— Ralph Waldo Emerson

Be what you want to be, not what others want
to see.
— Unknown

What the caterpillar calls the end of the world,
the master calls butterfly.
— Richard Bach

We cannot become what we need to be by
remaining what we are.
— Max De Pree

There is no end. There is no beginning. There is
only the passion of life.
— Federico Fellini

The habit of persistence is the habit of victory.
— Herbert Kaufman

Things worth having are worth waiting for.
— Paulo Coelho

Never give someone an opportunity to waste
your time twice.
— Unknown

Courage is facing your fears. Stupidity is Fearing
nothing.
— Todd Bellemare

The way we choose to see the world creates the
world we see.
— Barry Neil Kaufman

To be leader you must stand for something or
you will fall for anything.
— Anthony Pagano

When you're at the end of your rope, tie a knot
and hold on.
— Theodore Roosevelt

The only journey is one within.
— Rainer Maria Rilke

Be as you wish to seem.
— Socrates

We make our choices, then our choices make us.
— Unknown

If you fell down yesterday, stand up today.
— H. G. Wells

The noblest pleasure is the joy of understanding.
— Leonardo da Vinci

If everything seems under control, you're just not going fast enough.
— Mario Andretti

There is no elevator to success — you have to take the stairs.
— Zig Ziglar

Don't wait for opportunity, create it.
— Debasish Mridha

Nothing can disturb your peace of mind unless you allow it to.
— Roy T. Bennett

Don't ruin a good today because of a bad
yesterday.
— Unknown

Strength does not come from physical capacity.
It comes from an indomitable will.
— Mahatma Gandhi

Nothing can disturb your peace of mind unless
you allow it to.
— Roy T. Bennett

The secret of getting ahead is getting started.
— Mark Twain

Don't let what you cannot do interfere with
what you can do.
— John R. Wooden

The more you learn, the more you earn.
— Warren Buffett

Be proud of who you are, and not ashamed of
how someone else sees you.
— Unknown

Motivation comes from working on things we
care about.
— Sheryl Sandberg

Destiny is not a matter of chance, it is a matter
of choice. It is not a thing to be waited for, it is a
thing to be achieved.
— William Jennings Bryan

If you believe it will work out, you'll see
opportunities. If you believe it won't, you will
see obstacles.
— Wayne Dyer

Wisdom begins in wonder.
— Socrates

The best preparation for tomorrow is doing your
best today.
— H. Jackson Brown, Jr.

Great works are performed not by strength, but
perseverance.
— Dr. Samuel Johnson

Be the reason someone smiles today.
— Roy T. Bennett

If you do what you always did, you will get what you always got.
— Unknown

Either write something worth reading or do something worth writing.
— Benjamin Franklin

The question isn't who is going to let me; it's who is going to stop me.
— Ayn Rand

Time is what we want most, but what we use worst.
— William Penn

Live your beliefs and you can turn the world around.
— Henry David Thoreau

Believe you can and you're halfway there.
— Theodore Roosevelt

Don't wish it were easier. Wish you were better.
— Jim Rohn

The only person you are destined to become is
the person you decide to be.
— Ralph Waldo Emerson

Don't miss the Now.
— Unknown

If you want to change the fruits, you will first
have to change the roots.
— T. Harv Eker

Be sure to taste your words before you spit
them out.
— Auliq Ice

The problem is not the problem. The problem is
your attitude about the problem.
— Captain Jack Sparrow

Start every day with a smile and get it over with.
— W. C. Fields

There are essentially two things that will make us wiser: the books we read and people we meet.
— Charles Jones

You may have to fight a battle more than once to win it.
— Margaret Thatcher

Once you stop chasing the wrong things the right ones catch you.
— Lolly Daskal

The discipline of desire is the background of character.
— John Locke

Knowledge is knowing a tomato is a fruit; wisdom is not putting it in a fruit salad.
— Miles Kington

Deal with your problems before they deal with your happiness.
— Unknown

Mistakes are the portals of discovery.
— James Joyce

If you never try, you'll never know what you are
capable of.
— John Barrow

What consumes your mind, controls your life.
— Cait Flanders

Climb the mountain so you can see the world,
not so the world can see you.
— David McCullough Jr

Don't go through life, grow through life.
— Eric Butterworth

You can't have a million-dollar dream with a
minimum-wage work ethic.
— Stephen C. Hogan

It is better to sleep on things beforehand than
lie awake about them afterwards.
— Baltasar Gracian

Happiness is not the absence of problems; it's the ability to deal with them.
— Steve Maraboli

No matter what people tell you, words and ideas can change the world.
— Robin Williams

Consult not your fears, but your hopes and your dreams.
— Pope John XXIII

If the plan doesn't work change the plan but not the goal.
— Unknown

It's not the time you put in, but what you put in the time.
— Vince Lombardi

There is no more neutrality in the world. You either have to be part of the solution, or you're going to be part of the problem.
— T. Siedner

The two most important days in your life are the day you are born and the day you find out why.
— Mark Twain

There are no traffic jams along the extra mile.
— Roger Staubach

The ones who are crazy enough to think they can change the world, are the ones that do.
— Unknown

Be who you are and say what you feel, because those who mind don't matter, and those who matter don't mind.
— Bernard M. Baruch

The truth will set you free. But first, it will piss you off.
— Gloria Steinem

Challenges are gifts that force us to search for a new center of gravity. Don't fight them. Just find a new way to stand.
— Oprah Winfrey

You are always free to change your mind and choose a different future, or a different past.
— Richard Bach

Success is the sum of small efforts, repeated day-in and day-out.
— Robert Collier

Travelers, there is no path, paths are made by walking.
— Antonio Machado

You can't go back and change the beginning, but you can start where you are and change the ending.
— C.S. Lewis

An investment in knowledge always pays the best interest.
— Benjamin Franklin

Our attitude towards others determines their attitude towards us.
— Earl Nightingale

Opportunity doesn't knock, it presents itself
when you beat down the door.
— Kyle Chandler

If you can't stop thinking about it, don't stop
working for it.
— Michael Jordan

All that we see or seem is but a dream within a
dream.
— Edgar Allan Poe

The surest way to make your dreams come true
is to live them.
— Roy T. Bennett

Keep your face always toward the sunshine, and
shadows will fall behind you.
— Walt Whitman

Spread love everywhere you go.
— Mother Teresa

Limit your "always" and your "nevers".
— Amy Poehler

Your time is limited, so don't waste it living someone else's life.
— Steve Jobs

Don't limit your challenges, challenge your limits.
— Jerry Dunn

You must do the things you think you cannot do.
— Eleanor Roosevelt

Don't wait. The time will never be just right.
— Napoleon Hill

Life is like riding a bicycle. To keep your balance, you must keep moving.
— Albert Einstein

It isn't where you came from. It's where you're going that counts.
— Ella Fitzgerald

Self-discipline is when your conscience tells you to do something and you don't talk back.
— W. K. Hope

Try to be a rainbow in someone else's cloud.
— Maya Angelou

There will come a time when you believe
everything is finished. That will be the
beginning.
— Louis L'Amour

Don't miss out on your life just because you are
too busy scrolling through someone else's.
— Mell Robbins

The bad news is time flies. The good news is
you're the pilot.
— Michael Altshuler

You play like you practice and practice how you
play.
– Marcus Luttrell

Love all, trust a few, do wrong to none.
—William Shakespeare

Knowing yourself is the beginning of all wisdom.
—Aristotle

We lose ourselves in the things we love. We find ourselves there, too.
—Kristin Martz

Always forgive your enemies; nothing annoys them so much.
—Oscar Wilde

Nothing is more expensive than a missed opportunity.
— H. Jackson Brown

Fortune knocks but once, but misfortune has much more patience.
— Laurence J. Peter

A will finds a way.
— Orison Swett Marden

Don't cry because it's over, smile because it happened.
— Dr. Seuss

Remember that not getting what you want is
sometimes a wonderful stroke of luck.
—Dalai Lama

People who do not understand your silence will
probably not understand your words.
— Elbert Hubbard

Be your own Guru.
— Abhijit Naskar